Squeak, Squeal, Squawk

Luana K. Mitten

www.rourkepublishing.com

www.rourkepublishing.com

PHOTO CREDITS: Title Page: © Martinedegraaf; Page 4: © KeithJSmith; Page 6: © Jsalonis; Page 8: © nojustice; Page 10: © digitalg; Page 12: © Robert Ranson; Page 14: © digihelion; Page 16: © EkaterinaStarshaya; Page 18: © Ankevanwyk; Page 20: © Rmarmion; Page 21: © Jennifer Hogan, © Iofoto, © Stevieg999, © Andres Rodriguez; Page 22: © nojustice, © Ekaterina Starshaya, © digitalg, © Robert Ranson; Page 23: © digihelion, © KeithJSmith, © Jsalonis, © Ankevanwyk

Editor: Meg Greve

Cover design by Nicola Stratford, Blue Door Publishing

Page design by Teri Intzegian

Library of Congress Cataloging-in-Publication Data

Mitten, Luana K.
  Squeak, squeal, squawk / Luana Mitten.
     p. cm. -- (Animal babies and me)
Includes bibliographical references and index.
  ISBN 978-1-61590-261-3 (Hard Cover) (alk. paper)
  ISBN 978-1-61590-501-0 (Soft Cover)
1. Space perception--Juvenile literature. I. Title.
  BF469.M5845 2011
  591.3'9--dc22
                           2010010105

Rourke Publishing
Printed in the United States of America, North Mankato, Minnesota
033010
033010LP

www.rourkepublishing.com - rourke@rourkepublishing.com
Post Office Box 643328 Vero Beach, Florida 32964

Sneak-a-listen.

SQUEAK,
SQUEAK,
SQUEAK!

I hear . . .

a little **mouse**.

4

Sneak-a-listen.

SQUEAL,
SQUEAL,
SQUEAL!

I hear . . .

a little **pig**.

Sneak-a-listen.

SQUAWK, SQUAWK, SQUAWK!

I hear . . .

a little **bird**.

Sneak-a-listen.

CHIRRUP, CHIRRUP, CHIRRUP!

I hear . . .

a little **cricket**.

Sneak-a-listen.

RIBBIT, RIBBIT, RIBBIT!

I hear . . .

a little **frog**.

Sneak-a-listen.

mew,
mew,
mew!

I hear . . .

a little **kitten**.

Sneak-a-listen.

CHEEP, CHEEP, CHEEP!

I hear . . .

a little **chick**.

Sneak-a-listen.

YIP, YIP, YIP, YIP, YIP!

I hear . . .

a little **puppy**.

Sneak-a-listen.

YACKITY, YACK!

WEEEE!

YIPPEE!

I hear . . .

my friends playing
at the park!

Picture Glossary

bird (BURD): An animal with two legs, wings, feathers, and a beak.

chick (CHIK): A very young chicken that is covered with soft down before it grows feathers.

cricket (KRIK-it): An insect that jumps like a grasshopper and makes a chirping sound.

frog (FROG): An animal that lives in or near the water with webbed feet and long back legs for jumping.

kitten (KIT-uhn): A cat that is not fully grown.

mouse (MOUSS): A small, furry animal with a long nose, pointed ears, and a long tail.

pig (PIG): A farm animal with short legs, hoofs, and a long snout used for digging.

puppy (PUHP-ee): A dog that is not fully grown.

Index

Websites

www.kids.nationalgeographic.com/Animals/

www.kidscom.com/cgi-bin/Animalgame/

www.nefsc.noaa.gov/faq/index.html

About the Author

Luana Mitten lives in Tampa, Florida with her family and their dogs, Tuesday and Lucy. She likes to sneak-a-listen and hear her son and his friends giggling and yackity, yacking when they're playing.